THE TIME DRAWS NEAR THE BIRTH OF CHRIST:
The moon is hid; the night is still;
The Christmas bells from hill to hill
Answer each other in the mist.

Four voices of four hamlets round,
From far and near, on mead and moor,
Swell out and fail, as if a door
Were shut between me and the sound:

Each voice four changes on the wind,
That now dilate, and now decrease,
Peace and Goodwill, Goodwill and Peace,
Peace and Goodwill to all mankind.

Alfred Tennyson

George Mackley · wood engraver

When icicles hang by the wall,
    And Dick the shepherd blows his nail,
And Tom bears logs into the hall,
    And milk comes frozen home in pail,
When blood is nipp'd, and ways be foul,
Then nightly sings the staring owl,
            To-whit !
To-who !—a merry note,
While greasy Joan doth keel the pot.

When all aloud the wind doth blow,
    And coughing drowns the parson's saw,
And birds sit brooding in the snow,
    And Marian's nose looks red and raw,
When roasted crabs hiss in the bowl,
Then nightly sings the staring owl,
            To-whit !
To-who !—a merry note,
While greasy Joan doth keel the pot.

William Shakespeare.

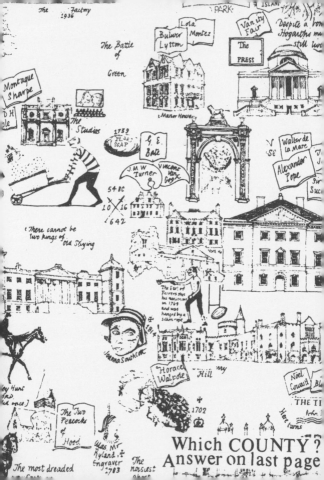

Which COUNTY?
Answer on last page

Goon! Ask the poor chap up.

1¼ lb. suet.
¼ lb. demerara sugar.
1 lb. raisins.
½ lb. sifted flour.
1 lb. eggs (weighed in their shells)
1 wineglassful brandy.
½ pint milk.

1 teaspoonful mixed spice.
½ teaspoonful nutmeg.
1 lb. breadcrumbs.
1 lb. sultanas.
4 oz. citron peel.
4 oz. candied peel.

The Royal Family's Christmas Pudding
Sufficient for twenty to twenty- eight people.

I am a Government Health Warning

AND THE COROLLARY of pAGe 6 maY be THIS

E'ER MORn ---

AND
aw
said on
Bethleh
pass, w
us. A
and Jo
And wh
abroad
ing this
dered a
the she
and po

A-men.

ame to pass, as the angels were gone
rom them into heaven, the shepherds
o another, Let us now go even unto
, and see this thing which is come to
n the Lord hath made known unto
hey came with haste, and found Mary
n, and the babe lying in a manger.
they had seen it, they made known
saying which was told them concern-
ild. And all they that heard it won-
nose things which were told them by
rds. But Mary kept all these things,
red them in her heart.

The King James Bible.

SYDNEY SMITH

This is the man who coined "A square peg in a round hole", who, when urged by his doctor to take a daily walk on an empty stomach, asked "Whose?", who made the glorious assertion that a friend's idea of heaven was "eating pâtés de foie gras to the sound of trumpets". In fact (as Macaulay said) THIS IS THE SMITH OF SMITHS.

Curate of Netheravon, Wiltshire:

"I have no relish for the country: it is a sort of healthy grave".

Editor of the Edinburgh

"I never read a book before reviewing it; it prejudices a man so,"

"The Scythians always ate their grandfathers: they behaved very respectfully to them for a long time but as soon as they became old and troublesome and began to tell long stories, they ate them."

Rector of Foston-le-Clay, Yorkshire

"There is not the least use of preaching to anyone unless you chance to catch them ill."

"He deserves to be preached to death by wild curates."

"How can a bishop marry? How can he flirt? The most he can say is 'I will see you in the vestry after service'."

"Marriage resembles a pair of shears, so joined that they cannot be separated, often moving in opposite directions, yet punishing anyone who comes between them."

"Heat, ma'am! Heat! It was so dreadful here that I found there was nothing for it but to take off my flesh and sit in my bones."

"What is real piety? What is true attachment to the Church? How are fine feelings best evinced? The answer is plain—by sending strawberries to a clergyman."

Canon of St. Paul's Cathedral.

"You might as well try to warm St. Paul's as warm the County of Middlesex."

"St. Paul's is certain death. My sentences are frozen as they come out of my mouth and are thawed in the course of summer, making strange noises and unexpected assertions in various parts of the church."

"When a child, stroking a tortoise, told me he was doing it 'to please it', I said that I now felt inspired to stroke the dome of St. Paul's so as to please the Dean and Chapter."

He was hardly ever unoccupied. When not reading, he was keeping up correspondence. A woman friend who had complained of low spirits, kept this list of his cures.

1. *Live as well as you can.*
2. *Go to the shower-bath with a low temperature.*
3. *Read amusing books.*
4. *Take a short view of life—no further than dinner or tea.*
5. *Be as busy as you can.*
6. *See as much as you can of friends that respect and like you.*
7. *and those acquaintances who amuse you.*
8. *Make no secret of low spirits but talk of them freely.*
9. *Attend to the effects coffee and tea produce on you.*
10. *Compare your lot with other people's.*
11. *Don't expect too much of life.*
12. *Avoid poets, dramatic presentations, music, serious novels, melancholy, sentimental people.*
13. *DO GOOD.*
14. *Be as much as you can in the open air.*
15. *Make your room gay.*
16. *Struggle by little and little against idleness.*
17. *Don't underestimate yourself.*
18. *Keep good blazing fires.*
19. *Be firm and constant in the exertion of rational religion.*

Riddles

LITTLE Nancy Etticoat,
With a white petticoat,
And a red nose;
She has no feet or hands,
The longer she stands
The shorter she grows.

Q. A thing with a thundering breech
It weighing a thousand welly,
I have heard it roar
Louder than Guys wild boar,
They say it hath death in its belly.

Q. Tho' of great age
I'm kept in a Cage
Having a long tail and one
ear,
My mouth it is round
And when Joys do abound
O' then I sing wonderful clear.

Once hairy scenter did transgress,
Whose dame, both powerful and fierce,
Tho' hairy scenter took delight
To do the thing both fair and right,
Upon a Sabbath day.

I'M called by the name of a man,
Yet am as little as a mouse;
When winter comes I love to be
With my red target near the house.

An old Woman whipping her Cat for Catching Mice on a Sunday.

I SING of a maiden
  That is makeless.
King of all kinges
  To her son she chose.

He came all so stille
  There his mother was
As dew in Aprille
  That falleth on grass.

He came all so stille
  To his mother's bower,
As dew in Aprille
  That falleth on the flower

He came all so stille
  There his mother lay,
As dew in Aprille
  That falleth on the spray.

Mother and maiden
  Was never none but she;
Well may such a lady
  Godes mother be.

54 NAMES BEGIN WITH C.   Answers INSIDE BACK COVER

VICTORIAN PLAYBILL GRAND CHRISTMAS
PERFORMANCE OF

THE SAILOR'S RETURN

THE OXEN

Christmas Eve, and twelve of the clock,
   "Now they are all on their knees,"
An elder said as we sat in a flock
   By the embers in hearthside ease.

We pictured the meek mild creatures where
   They dwelt in their strawy pen,
Nor did it occur to one of us there
   To doubt they were kneeling then.

So fair a fancy few would weave
   In these years! Yet, I feel,
If someone said on Christmas Eve,
   "Come; see the oxen kneel

"In the lonely barton by yonder coomb
   Our childhood used to know,"
I should go with him in the gloom,
   Hoping it might be so.

Thos. Hardy